GRASSE
HISTORIC TOWN

VILLE DE GRASSE

Circuit Touristique
Voie Piétonne
Sens unique de circulation
1/3600e env.

© 2004 ACT - Tél. : 04 93 88 33 62 - act@act.fr

7. Place du Petit Puy
The former podium is Grasse's oldest square.
Notre-Dame du Puy Cathedral, a listed historic building (12th, 13th and 18th centuries), is a perfect example of the Romanesque style of Provence, its high, narrow nave vaulted with heavy ogives.
In the right aisle are several paintings by Rubens (Perolle bequest), including the "Crown of Thorns" and the "Christ Crucified" and in the Holly Sacrament Chapel is the "Washing of the Feet" by Fragonard. There are also painting by Brea, Subleyras, Charles Nègre and Gaillard.

8. Place Antoine Godeau

9. Place du 24 août
Formerly Place du Grand Puy, it was the city's first cemetery, with a breathtaking view over the countryside around Grasse.

10. The Hôtel de Ville (Town Hall) occupies the former Episcopal palace and its tower (12th, 13th, 14th & 17th centuries). Two late 12th century arches grace the ground floor ; the bishops' private chapel (12th century) is located on the first floor. In the inner courtyard stands a fountain symbolising the City of Grasse and the prestige of its perfume industry by Rabuis, a 19th century sculptor from Grasse.
Court of Honour of the Hôtel de Ville Panoramic view over the city, under restoration.

11. Rue de l'Évêché
Corbelled house (14th/15th centuries) and arched doorway (14th century).

reignuways.
At n°2 & 4 Place aux Aires, a 13th century ogive was found.
At n°14th & 15th-century window with colonnette and 18th century stairwell.
At n°16 Place aux Aires, the home of Lyle Taulanne has an inner courtyard with 14th and 15th century triform windows.
At n°27 Place aux Aires, Hôtel du Dauphin was long the city's only inn.
At the centre of the square is the Market Clock (1802).
At n°33 Place aux Aires, the Isnard home, with a fine wrought-iron balcony, was built in 1781. Isnard was a rich tanner and merchant, father of Maximin Isnard, a remarkable Revolutionary orator and Girondist member of the Convention.

19. Place aux Aires, famous Provençal market every morning.

20. Rue Amiral de Grasse
At n°1, Hôtel Court de Fontmichel (since 1774), former Hôtel de Théas, dates from the 17th century. The rooms are decorated with paintings from Goethe's birthplace in Frankfurt, made at the request of the Count de Théas Thorenc, who represented King Louis XV there in 1759.

21. Square Fragonard or Square du Clavecin.

22. Mémorial Amiral de Grasse (Naval Museum).

23. Convention Centre, Cours Honoré Cresp, a late 19th century building, the former municipal casino. This is where Gérard Philipe, a famous stage and cinema actor from Grasse, began his career.

G. Rue Repitrel
14th century house.

H. Rue Tracastel (Retro Castellum)
It is located outside the mediaeval city's original urban nucleus, made up originally of Place du Petit Puy and Place du Grand Puy, the Bishop's palace and the Cathedral.
Chapelle Saint-Thomas (17th century) is a rare and remarkable example of the Baroque style of Provence.

I. Place de la Poissonnerie
The former fish market.

J. Place des Sœurs
At n° 11, Hôtel Russan de Thorenc is a former notable's house (14th century).

K. Place de la Fontette

L. Place de la Foux
This is where the city's main spring supplying water to the main wash houses and tanner's workshops in Grasse.

ARTISTLAND
Place of "Poissonnerie" and Place "Roustan"
"An inevitable meeting for art lovers, so magic, colors and sculpture lovers".
Nowadays, the artists are opening their spaces and they offer you all a year to share their passion....

The TARN and the JONTE GORGES.

"The first time I came in contact with the Tarn Gorges was on the 15th of September 1883.
In spite of the most enthusiastic descriptions I had read, reality far surpassed the dreams of my imagination.
Nowhere has nature edified a more extraordinary monument."

E.A. MARTEL

Les Détroits

F O R W A R D

To the South of the Massif Central on the edge of the Cevennes region, are the Causse moors.

Relatively high in altitude (about 1000 metres), the landscape is particularly dry and arid. Due to its numerous fissures, limestone soaks up rainwater very rapidly, so water is rare on the surface of the moors. On the other hand, it flows abundantly underground in a vast network hollowed out by streams and rivers at the bottom of the gorges. The original plateau has thus been cut into separate blocks divided by the rivers themselves.

The constant erosion caused by the water has resulted in the formation of the deep valleys of the Lot, Tarn, Jonte and Dourbie and their tributaries, as well as the caverns and chasms (avens) dug out in the limestone of the moors. The most impressive "canyon" is undoubtedly the Tarn valley, hewn out between Sauveterre moor to the north and Méjean moor to the south. Even so, the Jonte gorges and others such as the Dourbie and Trévezel are comparable and they are well worth a special excursion.

From the top of these moors, the view is just as impressive and anyone who enjoys walking can take unforgettable hikes along the cliff-top paths of Méjean or Causse Noir moors as well as taking the time to visit Aven Armand cavern, Bramabiau chasm and Dargilan caves. Just a few hours are necessary to discover the wonders of the underground world.

Nearby, Aigoual massif is also worth a visit. It contrasts sharply with the moors in its lush greenness and offers a beautiful view over the entire south of France, the Alps and the Pyrénées.

We suggest three road circuits (map and summary on page 2 of cover), which will enable an overall visit of the main sites of the region.

■ **THE TARN GORGES CIRCUIT** (circuit 1, in red on the map), the "royal path" between Florac and Le Rozier on the D907 road.

We strongly recommend you leave the canyon at least three times:
- at Saint Enimie to visit the lookout at St Chély cirque, on the Meyrueis road.
- at La Malène to go to Roc des Hourtous on Méjean moors.
- at Les Vignes to visit the Point Sublime.

Finally, you should take a canoe or boat trip down the river between La Malène and Les Baumes, which enables you to discover breathtaking views of the most spectacular part of the canyon, that cannot be seen from the road. This is an unforgettable experience and it would be a pity to miss it.

■ **THE COMPLETE CIRCUIT FROM LE ROZIER TO MEYRUEIS** (circuit 2, green-brown on the map) via Montpellier le Vieux, Millau, the **DOURBIE GORGES**, Mount Aigoual and Bramabiau

■ **THE JONTE GORGES** and the underground wonders of **AVEN ARMAND** and **DARGILAN** (circuit 3, green on the map).

These circuits can of course be adapted according to the time you have or your interests. You could for example, do the circuit from Méjean moors to Florac via Perjuret pass or cross it from Meyrueis to St Enimie or Les Vignes, which gives you a glimpse of life on the moors. (See page 52).

The best way to see the area however is to go hiking over the numerous way marked paths. The hike along the Tarn and Jonte cliff-tops from Le Rozier (see p3 from cover), is a must for those who enjoy a thrill.

This illustrated guide will facilitate your visit to a magnificent region. We have avoided all unnecessary description in a booklet that is first and foremost practical. On the other hand, we have largely illustrated it, believing that photos give a better idea of the landscape than words and that the guide will be a loyal souvenir of the trip you are about to take.

La Caze castle

MENDE, situated to the north.

Prefecture of the Lozère department and former capital of the Gévaudan region, Mende is situated on the banks of the Lot, at the foot of Mount Mimat, which rises up overlooking the city. Mende was built and developed around the tomb of Saint Privat, the first evangelist in the area, martyrized by the Barbarians in the 3rd century. During the suzerainty of Lord of Mende, the bishop at the time, the Hundred Years War took its toll on the city and was followed by the Wars of Religion. From the 19th century on, it became a large administrative centre.

Statue of Pope Urbain V

All that remains of the former ramparts is the Tour des Pénitents (12th century) on Soubeyran Boulevard. The old part of the city has recently been well restored and the picturesque lanes feature old fountains (le Griffon, la Caille, la Calquière), as well as pretty houses and private residences decorated with elegant doors.

photo G. Coural

Notre Dame bridge

Of particular interest is Notre Dame bridge (12th century), which spans the Lot, as well as Notre Dame and Saint Privat Cathedral. Rebuilt in the early 17th century, it is distinguished by its façade featuring two beautiful towers. Inside, the choir is remarkably decorated with 8 Aubusson tapestries from the early 18th century and in a luminous chapel to the left at the back of the church, is a very old statue of the Black Virgin. The lateral chapels, the crypts (featuring Saint Privat,s tomb) and the Sacristy are all of interest.

A huge bell clapper of 2.35 metres, originally part of Non Pareille bell, which was destroyed in 1579, can be seen near the cathedral entrance. There is a western door onto Urbain V square which features a statue of Pope Urbain V (born in 1309, 45 kms from Mende).

Rodez warrants a fuller description than can be allowed for here. Even so, in passing through the city, you should visit the cathedral, an admirable Gothic construction of stylistic unity from the 13th century onwards. It is of overall interest, in particular, the great tower (87 metres), next to the chevet and whose flamboyantly ornamented upper levels contrast with the simplicity of the lower sections.

The gate to the Aveyron region, Sévérac le Château is situated at the crossroads of the main traffic routes and was one of the richest towns of Rouergue. The fine archaeological museum shows ample evidence of its flourishing past. At the foot of the imposing fortress, the mediaeval streets feature beautiful 14th and 15th century residences.

Rodez

Sévérac le Château

SAINT AFFRIQUE, ROQUEFORT AND MILLAU , situated to the south.

Saint Affrique

A large commercial centre in the South Aveyron, SAINT AFFRIQUE was a Protestant stronghold during the wars of religion and valiantly resisted a siege by the army of Condé in 1628. The church with its soaring spire overlooks the narrow streets of the old city. Four bridges cross the Sorgues river, notably the Pont Vieux with its three humped arches. Caylus Rock overlooks the "seven hill city" and amongst the numerous dolmens counted nearby, Tiergues is the most famous.

ROQUEFORT-sur-Soulzon is situated on the flanks of the Combalou limestone cliffs, which in collapsing formed a network of fissures called "fleurines". These geological "flaws" are ideal for the ventilation of the cellars in which the famous Roquefort cheeses are matured. One of the cellars is open to the public and the archaeological museum in Roquefort shows evidence of man's presence on the site since Prehistoric times.

Roquefort cheese cellars

General view from the Larzac moors.

Situated at the confluence of the Dourbie and the Tarn, **MILLAU** is the busiest tourist centre in the Grands Causses region. The city takes its origins from Ancient Rome.

In the first century of our era, ancient Condatomagus was a centre for the manufacture of stamped pottery, which was exported all over the Roman Empire. Excavations undertaken south of the city on the site of Graufesenque have enabled us to reveal the fabrication techniques and numerous examples of pottery are exhibited in Millau museum.

Seat of a viscounty in the Middle Ages, Millau successively came under the protection of the counts of Provence, the Kings of Aragon, then the counts of Toulouse before finally being annexed to the French Crown in the 13th century. The religious wars wreaked havoc on this Protestant stronghold in the 16th century, destroying a large part of its architectural heritage. From the Middle Ages onwards, the city developed and expanded due to the skin and glove manufacturing industry which reached its height in the 18th century.

The former ramparts have become shady boulevards encircling the picturesque narrow streets of the old city. Notre Dame church, an old Romanesque edifice and the archaeological museum in Hôtel de Pégayrolles residence are situated near Foch square, a former Place d'Armes (military square), which has preserved its covered arches.

Overlooking the old section of the city is the belfry with its 12th century square tower and 17th century octagonal storeys. It is a vestige of the former town hall. Also worth visiting are the skin and glove museum housed in Hôtel de Tauriac, Saint Martin church, the old public washhouse, Sambucy castle and the remains of the old mediaeval bridge over the Tarn which still features a 15th century mill.

At the heart of the city, Mandarous square is highly animated in the summer season. Holidaymakers enjoy the sunny terrace cafés and hang-gliding amateurs gather while awaiting the right moment to take off and conquer the skies of Millau.

Millau viaduct (2004), work of the English architect Norman Foster, is the highest in the world (343metres).

Maréchal Foch square

The old mill

18th century public washhouse

FLORAC AND THE CEVENNES, situated to the east.

At the foot of Méjean moors, Florac is situated on the left bank of the Tarnon, close to its confluence with the Tarn. It was the capital of one of the eight baronies of Gévaudan. The castle features two round towers with steeply sloping roofs and has been the headquarters of the Cévennes National Park since 1970. It is pleasant to take a walk along the pretty shady esplanade and through the old streets where you can catch glimpses of the strange rock shapes on the edge of the moors.

At the foot of Rochefort rock, the gushing waters of Pêcher spring bring the urban landscape to life and add a picturesque note to the town before flowing into the Tarnon.

Pêcher spring is one of the main resurgences of Méjean moors.

Florac castle (17th century)

The road along the Cévennes ridge winds through magnificent landscapes.

Saint Germain de Calberte, in the heart of the Cévennes.

Situated in the south of the Massif Central, the CEVENNES are comprised of wooded highlands divided into long ridges by deep valleys, whose southern slopes overlook the garrigue scrublands and plains covered in Languedoc vineyards.

Its varied climate, mountainous landscape and rich fauna and flora make this area an ideal destination for lovers of solitude and natural wonders. Very irregular in relief and relatively high (1200 to 1500 metres), the Cévennes are "mountains in the shower": the record rainfall is 416mm in 12 hours. Mount Aigoual is the wettest mountain in France.

THE TARN GORGES

From Ispagnac onwards to Le Rozier, the Tarn has no tributaries and is only supplied by resurgences, which mostly flow directly into it from the bordering moors.

In this section, the gorges are the most spectacular with sheer cliffs 400 to 500 metres high. The rocks are strangely jagged, contrasting in their bareness and colours, which vary from ochre, red and sometimes streaked with black, with the multiple greens of the vegetation growing along the banks of the torrent. There is a succession of impressive views, isolated hamlets, castles and belvederes.

Ispagnac

Ispaganac church and its Romanesque door (12th century)

Built on request of Pope Urbain V, Quézac bridge enabled pilgrims access to the sanctuary erected in the village.

The pretty church porch at Quézac (16th century).

From Florac we head for Mende and soon cross the Tarn at Pont-du-Tarn. On either side of the road, cliffs of more than 1000 metres overlook the valley; schist and granite to the right and the limestone cliffs of Méjean moors to the left.

In a verdant basin of fertile crops (orchards and vineyards), ISPAGNAC has been named "the garden of Lozère". You should stop to see the Romanesque style church whose transept contains an octagonal cupola.

You can cross the Tarn over the old Gothic bridge at QUEZAC where the church contains a Virgin formerly visited by pilgrims

After MOLINES, the valley winds around to the south to the hamlet of Chambonnet where the road cuts a passage through the rocks towards Castelbouc, Prades, and Sainte Enimie.

Naturally sparkling mineral water from Quézac.

THE LEGEND OF CASTELBOUC

In the time of the Crusades, a young and handsome lord of the castle remained the only member of his sex amongst all his female subjects. The Crusade dragged on and in the endeavour to satisfy all of the ladies'desires; he eventually became exhausted, fell ill and perished from his excess of gallantry. As his soul set forth into the sky, an enormous Billy goat (bouc) could be seen floating above the castle towers. This is how CASTELBOUC got its name.

Castelbouc castle overlooks the Tarn from the top of a rocky spur 60 metres high

Sainte Énimie

SAINTE ENIMIE

As pretty as a picture, Sainte Enimie is on a remarkable site at the crossroads of the Causse de Sauveterre and Causse Méjean routes. If you have little time, at least take a walk through the narrow streets and along the Tarn banks (fine example of an arched "dos d'âne" bridge). A longer stay will enable you to visit the environs, in particular the hermitage where Saint Enimie lived, according to tradition. She was a Merovingian princess who was cured of leprosy by the miraculous waters of Burle fountain and then founded a monastery from which the village supposedly originated.

Once upon a time... in the era of the Merovingian kings, there was a princess admired by all of the court for her great beauty and pious virtues. Enimie was the daughter of King Clotaire II and the sister of the future King Dagobert and had decided to devote her entire existence to God. One fine day, her father decided to marry his daughter to one of the great barons of the kingdom. Unable to contest her father's decision, the young princess implored the Lord to take away her beauty, which seemed the only solution. Shortly after, her prayer was granted and her body was horribly disfigured with leprosy.

After many months of suffering, an angel appeared and commanded her to travel to Gévaudan, a region where a miraculous spring would cure her.

Saint Enimie

After a long voyage accompanied by a large escort as was fitting for her rank, she came to a region of deep canyons. She was met by shepherds who told her of a fountain that flowed into the Tarn nearby. It was the fountain of Burle.

As soon as she bathed in its waters, all traces of her terrible affliction disappeared and as if by miracle, her beauty was restored. Nevertheless as the troop left the region, the symptoms of her leprosy returned. The princess realized that the Lord wished her to remain in this place and devote herself to converting the region to Christianity. She founded a convent and a monastery whose ruins can still be seen at the heights of the village.

An old street

The Hermitage chapel

A "calade" or paved street.

*The Romanesque church (12-13th centuries)
and the old village.*

The old bridge on the Tarn with the hermitage in the background.

SAINT CHELY du Tarn

On leaving Sainte-Enimie along the right bank of the Tarn, the road heads towards the cirque and village of St-Chély, one of the most curious sites in the Tarn Gorges. The village nestles in a curve of the left bank and is accessible by a single-arched bridge.

La Cénarète, a small chapel in the centre of the village is dedicated to the Virgin.

Originating from a spring in the limestone, a stream flows through the village and cascades 10 metres into the Tarn.

Accessible from the Sainte Enimie - Meyrueis road, a trip up to the lookout is a must. There is a magnificent view over the village and the St Chély and Pougnadoires cirques.

St Chély cirque from the lookout.

La Cénarète chapel.

St Chély du Tarn.

After passing through Pougnadoires cirque, you come to La Caze castle, a fortified 15th century manor that has been converted into a hotel while preserving its mediaeval character. The inside and furnishings are in keeping with the style of construction.

The Nymph's Room in the south tower, with its eight portraits of the "Demoiselles de Malian" is a reminder of the eight damsels named the "Nymphes du Tarn", reputed for their charm and beauty.

As we continue southwards, we pass by the hamlet of Hauterive whose feudal castle in ruins overlooks the left bank, and come to La Malène.

Pougnadoires cirque.

La Caze castle (15th century).

On the left bank of the Tarn, Hauterive hamlet is only accessible by boat.

Going down the river by canoe.

The "Eiffel Tower" at Pougnadoires.

A small village at the foot of a rocky spur on Sauveterre moors, La Malène is the starting point for the boat trip along the most spectacular part of the gorges to Les Baumes cirque.

The extraordinary Passage des Détroits (straits) can be best and most realistically appreciated only by boat, as it is indeed the most beautiful section of the entire gorges. From the road high up on the right bank of the canyon, it is impossible to see the narrowest and most impressive passage. At the end of the boat trip, a taxi will take you back to your car at La Malène. The taxi fee is included in the cost of the boat ride.

The flat-bottomed boats take 4 or 5 passengers and are expertly guided by boatmen through a succession of rapids ("ratchs") and peaceful pools ("planiols").

In the Détroits, the river flows between steep vertical cliffs 400 to 500 metres high where vegetation grows with difficulty. The rock faces are beautifully coloured with traces of mineral salts in long black streaks, highlighted with orange and ochre tints that glow in the sunlight.

You must also make a visit to the small Romanesque church and Montesquieu castle, which is nowadays a hotel.

General view of La Malène from the road on Méjean moors.

Since man has known how to build crafts, he has undoubtedly used the Tarn to travel from one village to another or to tend to his crops along the river. This was the custom in the gorges until 1905, when construction on the road began. Even so, the first tourists, who were more like explorers, used boats to visit the Tarn canyon. Though tourist activity of this kind had begun towards 1880, 1905 is considered as the official beginning of the boat trips as such, with the signature of the first prefectorial order controlling navigation.

Until 1952, hotel owners organized the trips, then the boatmen joined up and formed a cooperative. Today, the boatmen's descendants still operate the cooperative in the form of a workers production company, maintaining the tradition of boat excursions in the Tarn gorges. The Malène boatmen will take you on a trip to discover the most beautiful part of the gorges between La Malène and Les Baumes cirque passing through the famous straits, Les Détroits, at the foot of 500 m high cliffs.

The 8 km excursion down the river is fully guided and commented by the boatman. It is also the best way to see the very particular fauna and flora of the gorges and discover a unique and fascinating landscape that the visitor will never forget.

Montesquieu castle with its small towers, at La Malène.

The spectacular hairpin bend road that descends from Méjean moors to La Malène.

The great cliff.

The "mushroom".

From La Malène, hairpin bends (photo upper left) take you to the Mejean moors.
From Hourtous Rock, there is a remarkable view over the gorges.

Les Détroits (The straits)

La Croze hamlet as you come out of Les Détroits.

The boat trip ends at Cirque des Baumes, more precisely at Baumes-Hautes, where the road also passes, after having wound under the overhanging cliff and through two tunnels. We are just beneath Point Sublime, but to get there by car you must drive up from Les Vignes village (see further on). You can also reach it on foot by climbing a path with steps (which takes about an hour). The cliff-side is pitted with caves. Under one of them and in front of the rock, you can see St-Ilère hermitage, where eye diseases were supposedly cured by the healing spring water in the cave behind the chapel.

Rock named "Christ's head".

St Ilère (or Hilaire) chapel.

Overhanging cliff.

Autumn mildness.

A view to the east from Point Sublime: Baumes Hautes, Les Détroits and Roc des Hourtous on the edge of the moors.

A view to the south from Point Sublime: Les Baumes Basses, Roche Aiguille, Pas de Soucy and Les Vignes cirque.

The Tarn at Pas de Soucy.

PAS DE SOUCY

The road goes on to Pas de Soucy, a pile of rocks that has tumbled down from the cliff forming a natural dam. The Tarn pushes its way through the rocks with difficulty and a magnificent view of the passage can be seen from the lookout at Roc de la Sourde.
A little further along the riverbank on the same side, Aiguille rock towers 80 metres high.

LES VIGNES

The village is situated on the right bank of the Tarn. On this side of the river, a winding road climbs up to Sauveterre moors. You leave it after 5 kms, turning right towards Point Sublime. You are more than 400 metres above the Tarn and have a magnificent view of the gorges and the moors.
Downstream from Les Vignes, the narrow canyon continues almost in a straight line, still with the same wild landscape until La Muse Bridge near the neighbouring towns of Le Rozier and Peyreleau.

Aiguille rock.

THE LEGEND OF ROQUE SOURDE

Satan was fleeing the moors pursued by Saint Enimie. As she came to the top of the cliff above the Tarn, she realized she could not catch the Evil one and called upon the giant rocks that surrounded her. An enormous landslide instantly answered her prayer and the huge ROQUE-SOURDE hurtled down towards the Devil. Unfortunately, he managed to squeeze into a crack in the bed of the Tarn and so escaped, bruised but safe, back to the Kingdom of Hell. The huge pile of rocks, named PAS de SOUCY was the result of the landslide.

Les Vignes.

Autumn adorns the gorges in an array of bright colours. The view from Pas de l'Arc, between Les Vignes and Le Rozie

The old hamlet of La Sablière clinging to the steep slopes of Cinglegros rock.

View of the canyon from the top of Cinglegros rock.

Baousso del Biel, a natural bridge 40 metres high,
27 metres under the arch and 25 metres wide.
It was hollowed out by one of the wandering arms
of the Tarn and is a remarkable example of early
erosion in the canyon.

Troglodyte dwellings at St Marcellin.

Peyreleau and the entrance to the Jonte gorges.

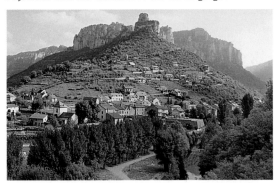

Le Rozier at the confluence of the Tarn and Jonte.

LE ROZIER and PEYRELEAU

At the confluence of the Tarn and the Jonte, Capluc rock stands out on the edge of Méjean moors.

The "twin towns" of LE ROZIER and PEYRELEAU, one in the Lozère department, the other in the Aveyron, nestle at the foot of the moor escarpments. Before coming to Le Rozier, you pass by its 12th century Romanesque church. There are Gallo-Roman potteries and an old christening font on display in the Presbytery.

The old houses of Peyreleau rise up in tiers over the slopes of Causse Noir moor, dominated by the church and an old crenellated tower.

2 kms downstream from Le Rozier, close to the Tarn and beneath the village of Mostuéjouls, there is a beautiful church, Notre Dame des Champs. Overall Romanesque in style, except for a Gothic chapel to the right of the nave, it features a bell-tower wall with 4 arches.

The near-by villages of Mostuejouls, Liaucous and Peyrelade are also worth a visit.

The remains of La Muse bridge, which was washed away when the river broke its banks in 1900.

The Romanesque church at Le Rozier.

Vase de Sevres, on one of the rocky ledges of the Jonte, which are renowned for rock climbing.

Notre Dame des Champs

Capluc Rock, also named "Tête de Lumière".

The DOURBIE gorges, Mont AIGOUAL and BRAMABIAU, via MILLAU.

This circuit enables you to visit the large natural sites in the environs of the Tarn gorges and explore the Cévennes at the summit of Mount Aigoual. In doing so, you travel up the entire Dourbie valley dotted with charming little villages. You can also visit Millau and see its famous aqueduct. The capital of the Causse moors region, Millau is the veritable entrance point to the gorges and is worth more than a passing halt.

From Peyreleau, you take the road to Causse Noir moor, which takes its name from the old pine forests, before coming to Montpellier le Vieux. Nearby, you can also visit two of the curious eroded rock formations, the "chaos" of Roquesaltes and Rajol.

T he rocky «chaos» of Montpellier le Vieux can be visited on foot; the easy, well-marked circuit takes about an hour and a half. Covering an area of 120 hectares, natural erosion has formed a collection of the most strangely shaped rocks. Their extraordinary silhouettes are reminiscent of the ruins of a legendary city.

At Maubert farm, take the same path to the left, which winds down across the moor to Millau (see p 10). Two thirds of the way along in a series of hairpin bends, there is a magnificent view of the Tarn, the city and the road viaduct, which spans the horizon.

Mycenae's gate at Montpellier le Vieux.

La Roque Sainte Marguerite.

NANT and ST JEAN du BRUEL

Crossing Cureplat bridge, you leave Millau and enter the Dourbie valley, which winds between Causse Noir moor on the left and Larzac moor on the right.

You come to Roque-Ste-Marguerite (access to Roquesaltes rock and Rajol chaos is easy from here), then St-Veran, with its picturesque houses in tiers along the cliff.

On the left you pass Cantobre with its old houses, many of which are in ruins, before coming to NANT. The town features a pretty 12th century church, a 14th century covered market, old houses and an interesting old bridge.

Continue following the Dourbie upstream to the pretty village of SAINT JEAN DU BRUEL, then go on towards Trèves. The river winds its way through granite rocks and you reach Espérou via Dourbie.

Instead of driving up the Dourbie gorges, you could alternatively continue northward after Pierre Plantée pass and follow Trévezel gorges to reach Camprieu via Trèves.

Corp mill.

At the confluence of the Trevezel and the Dourbie, Cantobre is situated on a promontory of Bégon moor.

The Dourbie in Autumn.

The wilderness of the Dourbie gorges.

General view of Nant.

St Pierre de Nant church.

St Jean de Bruel.

The observatory overlooking the Cévennes valleys, hidden in a sea of clouds.

MOUNT AIGOUAL (1567metres)

The drive up the Dourbie gorges has brought you to Serreyède pass (1302 metres), where the Hérault takes its source.

Near the pass to the east, you can go and see Hérault waterfall. We are now only a few kilometres from the summit of Mount Aigoual.

This magnificent belvedere on which a weather observatory was built in 1887, boasts a spectacular view, best seen from the viewpoint indicator erected right at the summit. The panorama stretches out from Mont Blanc to Pic d'Aneto with Puy de Sancy and the Mediterranean coast in between.

Among the many possible walks in the massif, we recommend Orgon cascade trail (from Espérou through the pass and Aulas mountain) and Hort-de-Dieu trail (Jardin de Dieu), beneath Aigoual summit, a 15-hectare Alpine garden near Valleraugue valley.

Trévezel gorges.

Before leaving the forests and returning to the aridity of the moors, you must stop at Bramabiau.

A small river, the Bonheur, flows down from Aigoual then disappears into a chasm in the Camprieu limestone plateau and cascades out the other side. It flows underground for 700 metres through a fissure at the foot of the cliff. When there is heavy rain and flooding, the waters make such a noise that they sound like the bellowing of an ox (brama-biau). Once you have left Bramabiau, the typical "causse" moors landscape reappears in striking contrast to that of the Aigoual massif.

Following the Bétuzon river, you come to Meyrueis.

MARTEL, THE FATHER OF SPELEOLOGY

Edouard Alfred Martel (1859-1938) is considered the "father" of modern speleology. His exploration of Bramabiau underground river on the 27th of June 1888 was the foundation act.

For 25 years, he explored most of the limestone regions of France and visited numerous caves in Europe and America. The various publications recounting his expeditions have largely contributed to the popularity of speleology and made it accessible to the public as well as developing tourism in the region. As early as 1883, he made a canoe trip down the Tarn gorges. The list of his exploration campaigns is too long to give here but we must mention the most well known in the region: Bramabiau and Dargilan (1888), Padirac (1889), Aven Armand (1897).

Martel's stele at Bramabiau.

The JONTE gorges
DARGILAN and AVEN ARMAND

MEYRUEIS is favourably situated at the confluence of the Jonte and two small streams, the Brèze and the Bétuzon. It is close to the Jonte gorges in a landscape which is half way between the limestone moors and the vegetation covered schist of the Aigoual massif.

The town is one of the most popular holiday centres for excursions to the Tarn gorges as well as the edge of the Cévennes and Mount Aigoual. Ramparts once encircled the old section of Meyrueis but today, all that remains is one round tower (Tour de l'Horloge) and a little further on, two city gates.

Outside the town and built on the top of a large rock, Notre Dame de Bon Secours chapel overlooks the houses from a height of 70 metres. Meyrueis is the centre of the triangle containing the underground wonders of the region. Dargilan and Aven Armand caves and Bramabiau chasm are only a few kilometres away.

General view of Meyrueis from the Sainte Enimie road.

Notre Dame du Rocher.

Six Liards bridge, a former toll bridge.

Les Bouillères rocks and tunnel.

51

The fox

DARGILAN, "the Pink Cavern"

A visit to Dargilan cave is alone worth an excursion. You can follow a well-marked itinerary for approximately 1.5 kms, which will give you a good overall view of this magnificent cavern of imposing proportions. Amazingly coloured concretions of the strangest shapes and forms abound, with evocative names such as The Draperies, The Mosque, Macaroni, The Bell-tower etc. According to legend, a young shepherd called Sahuquet discovered the caves while following a fox that had disappeared through a crack in the rock.

*"It is immense!.., superb!..,
magnificent!...
A real forest of stone.
It is splendid Mr. Martel,
there are over 100 columns..."*

It is in these words that Louis Armand described his wonderment to Martel, on discovering the cave that would bear his name.

An electric funicular is now used to descend into Aven Armand. 75 metres underground, we step out above a huge gallery 40 metres high and 50 to 100 metres wide. A path with steps in places enables you to walk around this prodigious natural museum containing the most extraordinary formations to be found in underground caverns: stalagmites, concretions of all shapes (The Palm Tree, The Cauliflowers, The Tiger's Jaws, The Calvary, The Virgin and Child, etc.).

It is a fairyland gallery whose dimensions are large enough to hold Notre Dame de Paris church!

The rocky ledges of Méjean moor on the Jonte side.

F ollow the right bank of the Jonte through the narrow gorges. Two layers of bare cliffs interspersed with vegetation-covered slopes rise up on either side. These terraced cliffs in tiers are unusual and are a special feature of the Jonte canyon.

After Sourgette mill, you come to Douzes Fountain, a spring originating from the Jonte. You then go on to Douzes hamlet, dominated by St-Gervais rock and its pretty chapel, Maynial hamlet on the left bank, and Le Truel with its lookout, Les Terraces.

Clinging to the top of the gigantic Méjean cliffs, Vase de Sèvres and Vase de Chine rocks suddenly appear, followed by Capluc rock before you get to Le Rozier. You can go from Peyreleau as far as the ruins of St-Jean-de-Balmes on the Causse Noir moor where you can easily get to Madasse cirque and Fabié and Curvelié rocks. Hiking trails run over the Causse Noir and Méjean moors.

The terraced cliffs at Le Truel.

Describing the Tarn gorges in 1894, Abbot Solanet wrote: "*The vultures of the region have taken up residence in this formidable fortress. They are here in myriads.*"

In the years that followed, their numbers were dramatically reduced and between 1930 and 1940, they disappeared entirely. Shot, poisoned and unable to find sufficient food, these great birds known as "nature's cleaners" were gradually wiped out. In the 1970's, the Cévennes National Park Foundation for Birds of Prey decided to reintroduce the Griffon or "tawny" vulture, an exceptional and unprecedented initiative. Between 1981 and 1986, about 60 birds were released and the colony is estimated to reach 110 reproductive couples in 2005. The operation was so successful that the European community entrusted the Cévennes National Park and the League for the Protection of Birds with the task of reintroducing another species: the Cinereous vulture. Begun in 1992, reintroduction of these birds has now increased their population to about 50. An emblematic species due to its rarity in Europe, the Cinereous vulture can only be observed in the Tarn and Jonte gorges.

1986 brought an unexpected surprise: 2 couples of Egyptian white-backed vultures returned spontaneously to the region. This was a welcome "gift" as there are no more than 70 couples remaining in France. Why has nature created 3 species of carrion feeders? Each species has a particular food preference:

- **The Griffon vulture** prefers soft tissue such as muscles and intestines.
- **The Cinereous vulture** feeds on hard flesh such as tendons, cartilage and skin.
- As for the **Egyptian vulture**, it arrives after the others and expertly cleans up the leftovers with its sharp, slender beak. These birds are exclusively necrophagous and are entirely dependant on the sheep farms of the Grands Causses moors in their search for food.

Their nesting sites are in the Tarn and Jonte gorges.

VULTURE BELVEDERE at Le Truel (Belvédère des Vautours)

Although it is relatively easy to see the birds in their natural habitat, it is more informative to visit Belvédère des Vautours, in the Tarn and Jonte gorges. An ideal spot, the site is particular in that it combines an exhibition recounting the adventure of vulture reintroduction and their biology, as well as an observation post equipped with telescopes and movie cameras focused on a nest, resting places and a feeding area. Direct observation of the birds'habits is thus made possible. The ornithologists at the Le Truel Belvedere des Vautours will be pleased to share their knowledge of and passion for vultures with you.

BELVÉDÈRE DES VAUTOURS   tél 05 65 62 69 69
LE TRUEL 48150 ST PIERRE des TRIPIERS   www.vautours-lozere.com

C. Bagnolini frees a young Cinereous vulture.

Young Cinereuos vulture.

"Europe", the first vulture chick born in its natural environment in France for over a century.

A group of Griffon vultures.

The path along the ridges at Pas du Loup: Vase de Chine (23 metres), Vase de Sèvres and Capluc rock.

Vase de Sèvres (21 metres), a popular rock climbing spot; in the background, Peyreleau village.

*"All paths ended in the sky, travelling still higher and higher,
towards destinations which no longer belonged to the earth but to a lost Celestial continent."*

Jean Carrière (La Caverne des Pestiférés)

THE GRANDS CAUSSES MOORS

The cardabelle thistle grows close to the ground on the moors. It is often hung on barn doors as a natural barometer. If the petals open, the weather will be fine; when they curl up, rain is in store.

Overlooking the Tarn and Jonte gorges are the Grands Causses moors: Sauveterre, Méjean, Causse Noir and Larzac. Man has always inhabited these arid, stony and windswept plateaus, largely contributing to the disappearance of the forests, which has given them their present day bare appearance. Cultivation of the land is concentrated in the "combes" and the "sotchs", small fertile basins dotting the Causses. Dairy sheep farming is the main agricultural activity, supplying the indispensable ewe's milk for the manufacture of Roquefort cheese. The white limestone and slate roofs of the traditional Causse farms blend into the surrounding countryside, whose charm is both simple and grandiose.

Light plays on the Causses, adding a touching note to the landscape. Typical plants found in the area include the cardabelle thistle, the anemone pulsatille or windflower and the spring Adonis. For several years now, the Griffon vulture has soared majestically above the moors.

photo Y.Cavaillé

A "lavogne", or small clay-lined pond, one of the rare waterholes in this arid region.

Hyelzas farm on Méjean moor, a symbol of Causse architecture.

"Aragon" style farm on Sauveterre moor.

Buffre cross (1151): 2 figures are carved on the base, which features a human head as a font. This is the oldest sculpted cross in Lozère.

Nîmes le Vieux.

Garlands of "angel hair" grass "ripple in the swell of a sparkling sea".

Spring Adonis.

The green lizard is commonly found on the moors.

Anemone pulsatille.

Spring on the moors.

Przewalski horses on Méjean moor are well adapted to the steppe landscape and harsh climate, which are not unlike the conditions in the land of their Mongolian ancestors.

Baumelle cave.

Saint Pierre arches.

Photographs

Jean-Paul **AZAM**
Claude **CARRIER**
Didier **POUX**
Philippe **POUX**

Layout, computer graphics:

Jean-Paul **AZAM**

English translation:

Nancy **KINZBRUNNER**

" It was this, the love of a country, the slight but exquisite suffering at the idea that a lifetime would not suffice to travel the length and breadth of its paths and to feast on its smallest furrows."

Jean **Carrière** (L'Epervier de Maheux)

APA POUX Editions - Albi
Translation, reproduction and adaptation rights
reserved for all countries.
Copyright March 2005
ISBN: 2 913641-46-6
Printed in the EC